How to Make Flibbers, etc.

A BOOK OF THINGS TO MAKE AND DO

by

Robert Lopshire

BEGINNER BOOKS A Division of Random House, Inc.

To my four favorite Flibber Makers,
Martin, Howard, Terry and Vicky.

This title was originally catalogued by the Library of Congress as follows: Lopshire, Robert. How to make flibbers, etc.; a book of things to make and do. (New York, Beginner Books, 1964). 61 p. col. illus. 24 cm. 1. Creative activities and seat work. I. Title. GV1201.L84. j793. 64—22011. ISBN 0-394-80037-0 ISBN 0-394-90037-5 (lib. bdg.)

How to Make Flibbers, etc.

How to Make
a
Zum Zum Fiddle

1 – Get a big
cardboard box.
Get some
strong string.

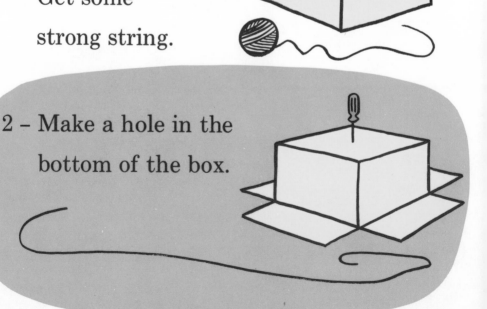

2 – Make a hole in the
bottom of the box.

3 – Tie a little stick
   on the end of the string.
   Pull the string through
   the hole in the box.

5 – Tie the string
   to a broom.

6 – Hold the broom
   like this . . .

. . . and make crazy music!

How to Make
Limp Lamps

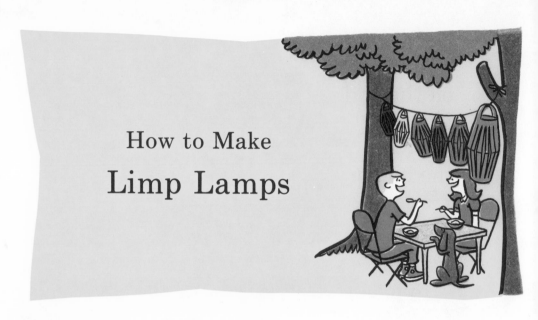

1 – Get a piece of paper
and some scissors.

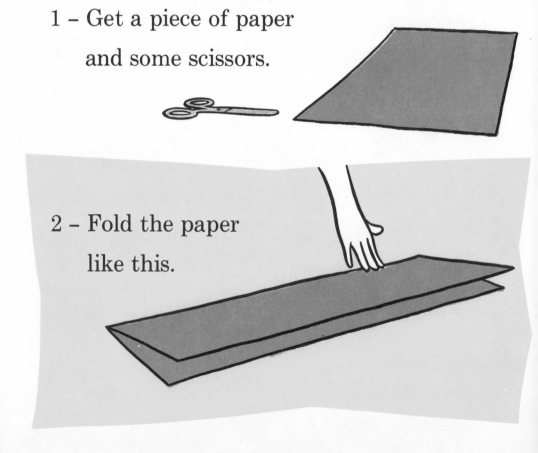

2 – Fold the paper
like this.

3 – Now cut the paper
   like this.

4 – Unfold the paper.
   Bend it around
   like this.
   Stick the two
   ends together.

5 – Cut another piece
   of paper. Stick it
   on for a handle.

Make a lot of Limp Lamps.
Hang them up. Have a party!

How to Make
a
Humdinger

1 – Get a button . . .
   a very big one.

2 – Find a piece of string.

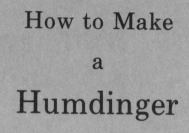

3 – Put the string
   in the button
   like this.

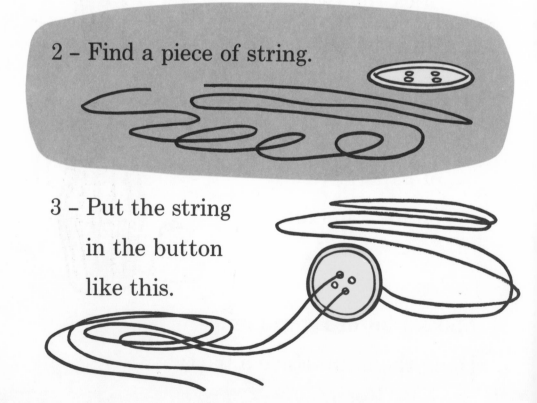

4 – Tie a knot
   in the string.

5 – Hold the string
    and twirl it.
    Wind it up.

6 – Then pull and let go.
    Pull HARD! And let go.

Keep it going.
It may go FOREVER!

How to Make

a

Flibber

1 – Get a newspaper.

Get an old one.

2 – Put three pieces

on the floor like this.

3 – Roll them up.

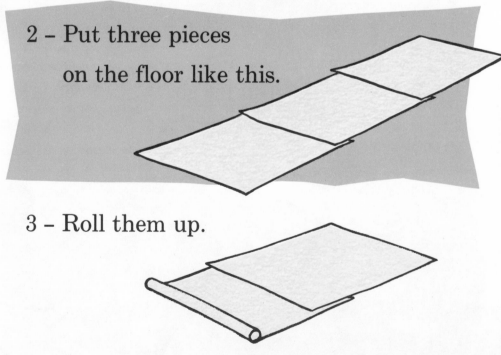

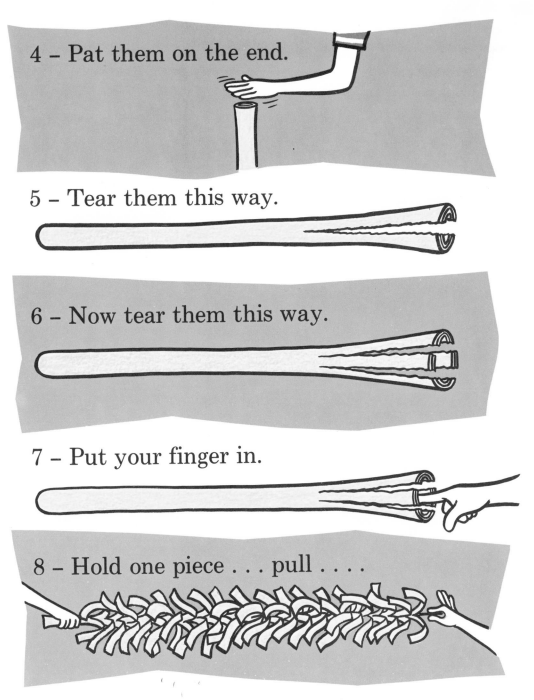

4 – Pat them on the end.

5 – Tear them this way.

6 – Now tear them this way.

7 – Put your finger in.

8 – Hold one piece . . . pull . . . .

And, now you have a Flibber!

How to Make

a

Sweet Pete

1 – Ask your mother
   for an orange,
   a toothpick,
   and some cloves.

2 – Take the toothpick.
   Make small holes
   in the orange
   for Pete's eyes, nose
   and mouth.

3 – Stick cloves
  in the holes.

4 – Now make holes
  for his hair.
  Make a lot of them.

5 – Stick more cloves
  in those holes.

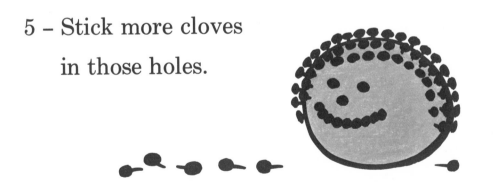

Keep Pete in your room.
He will make it smell fine!

How to Make
a
Whirligig

1 – Get a piece of paper.
   Get a bead, a pin,
   and a stick.

2 – Cut the paper
   four times
   like this.

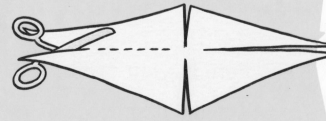

3 – Pull four pieces
   of the paper over
   like this.

4 – Put the pin through
   the paper like this.

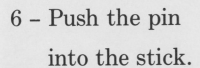

5 – Put the bead on the pin.

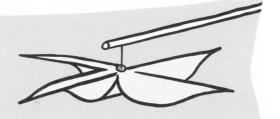

6 – Push the pin
   into the stick.

7 – Now go out and run.
   Make your Whirligig whirl!

How to Make
Party Mats

1 – All you need are
scissors and
two pieces
of colored paper.

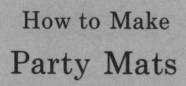

2 – Fold, and cut
one piece
like this.

3 – Cut the other
   piece into strips.

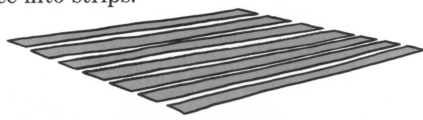

4 – Lay the first
   piece down flat.
   Take a strip and
   go over and under
   like this.

5 – Do this with
   all the strips.

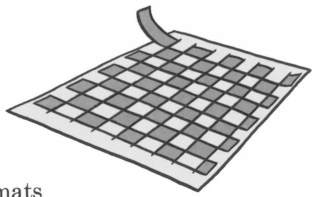

6 – Make a lot of mats
   and have a party.

How to Grow

a

Jungle

1 – Ask your mother
   for a sweet potato.

2 – Get four toothpicks
   and a glass of water.

3 – Put the toothpicks
   in the potato
   like this.

4 – Put the potato in
   the water like this.

5 – Keep it wet,
   and your Jungle
   will grow.

But be careful!
Look out for those tigers!

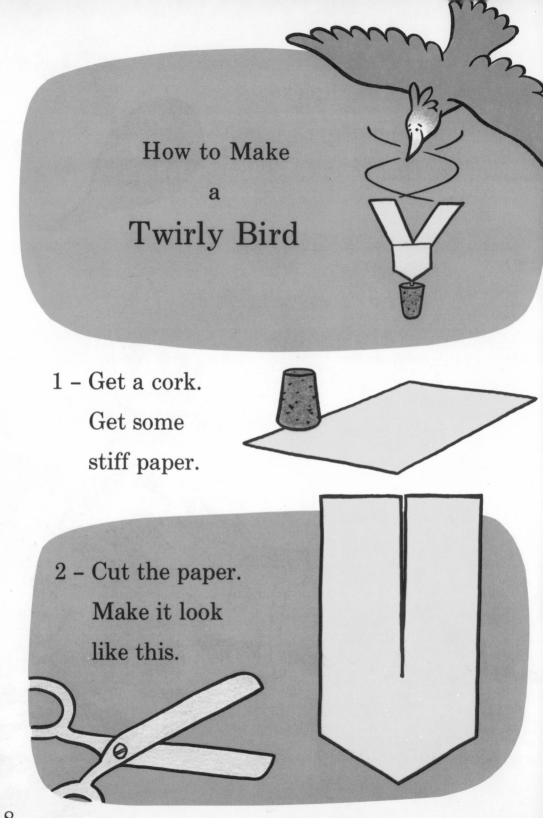

How to Make

a

Twirly Bird

1 – Get a cork.
Get some
stiff paper.

2 – Cut the paper.
Make it look
like this.

3 – Bend the paper
like this.

4 – Stick a toothpick
on the paper
with stickum.

5 – Now push
the toothpick
into the cork.

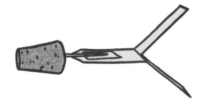

6 – Take your bird outside
and throw him in the air.

19

How to Make
a
Screecher

1 – Get some

paper.

2 – Cut a piece

of paper this big.

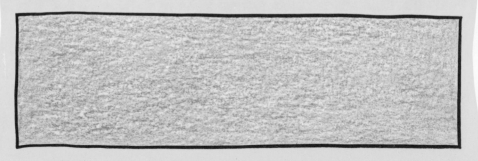

3 – Fold the paper
   and cut it
   like this.

4 – Fold it again.
   Make it look
   like this.

5 – Hold it up to
   your mouth
   this way.

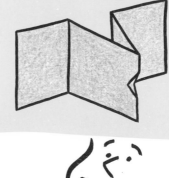

6 – Now blow!
   Blow hard!

You can call your friends
this way . . . .

21

How to Make

a

Yakky Pup

1 – Get a paper bag.

   Not too big.

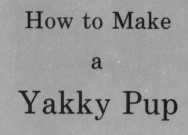

2 – Get some crayons, too.

3 – Draw a face like this.

4 – Draw the mouth here.

5 – Cut some ears out of paper.

6 – Color the ears
   and stick them on.

7 – Put your hand
   in the bag.
   Move your fingers
   and make him talk.

He will talk with you for hours!

How to Make
Potato Prints

1 – Ask your mother
     for a potato, a dish,
     some paper,
     and paint.

2 – Ask her to cut
     the potato in half.

3 – Have her cut
one half so it
looks like this.

4 – Put some paint
on the dish.
Dip the potato
in the paint.

5 – Now press the potato
down on the paper.
Do this all over
the paper.

What do you do with it now?
Turn the page and see . . . .

How to Make

a

Present for Dad

1 – Take your Potato Print

and a can

like this one.

2 – Cut the paper.
Cut off a piece
as wide as the can.

3 – Stick the paper
   around the can.

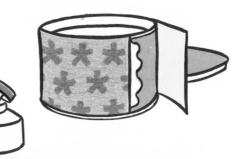

4 – Put the top
   of the can
   on the other piece.
   Draw around it.

5 – Now cut it out.

6 – Stick it on the can top.

Your dad will keep his money
and buttons and stuff in it.

How to Make

a

Phony Phone

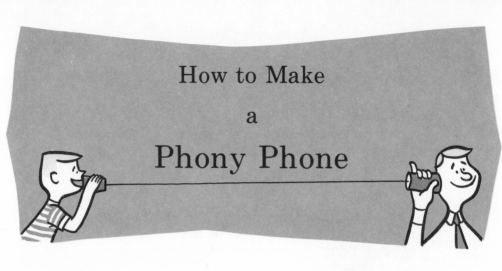

1 - Get two paper cups . . .

2 - . . . and a long piece of thread.

3 - Make a hole in each cup,

a very small pinhole.

4 – Pull the thread
   through the holes.

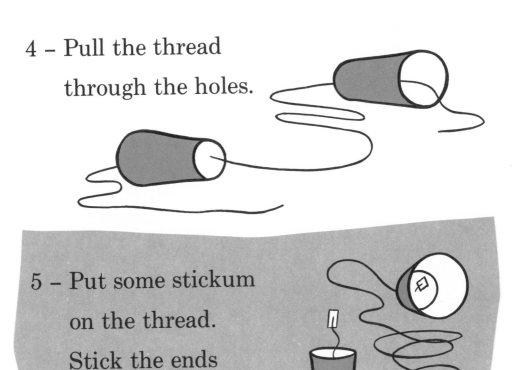

5 – Put some stickum
   on the thread.
   Stick the ends
   inside the cups.

6 – Pull the thread tight
   and talk into your cup.

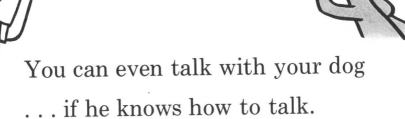

You can even talk with your dog
   . . . if he knows how to talk.

How to Make

a

Stickit Picture

1 – Get some cardboard,

scissors, and a

lot of colored paper.

2 – Cut the paper into

a zillion pieces.

3 – Stick the pieces
on the cardboard.
Have fun! Stick them
any way you want to.

4 – Stick and stick,
and stick and stick!

When it's done
your mother will
hang it in your room.

Now make one for Mother.

How to Make

a

Creepy Willy

1 – Get some paper.

Get your scissors.

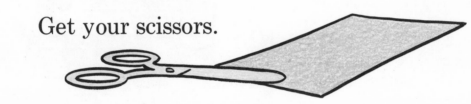

2 – Cut out a piece

of paper this big.

Draw his face on it.

3 – Pull him
over a table.
This will
make him curly.

4 – Wet Willy.
Not *too* wet.

5 – Put him on a table
and blow
on his tail.

Have a Creepy Willy race!

How to Make

a

Nip Bug

1 – Get a clothespin.
Get your scissors,
some colored paper,
glue and two tacks.

2 – Push the tacks
in the clothespin.
They are his eyes.

3 – Cut out some
paper legs and
glue them on.

4 – Cut out some wings.
Cut out a tail.
Color them
with funny dots.

5 – Glue on his wings
and tail like this.

6 – Open the Nip Bug's
nipper . . .

. . . and nip him on anywhere.

How to Make
a
Huffel Hat

1 – Get a paper cup,
a string and
some straws.

2 – Put the straws on
the string like this.

3 – Tie the string
around the straws.

4 – Make a hole
in the top
of the cup.

5 – Pull the string
through the hole.

6 – Tie the string
under your chin.

Your dog will think you are very pretty.

How to Make

a

Walking Thing

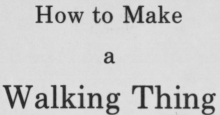

1 – Get a rubber band.
Get a spool and
two toothpicks.

2 – Rub some soap
on the spool.
Rub it on both ends.

3 – Put the rubber band
   through the hole.

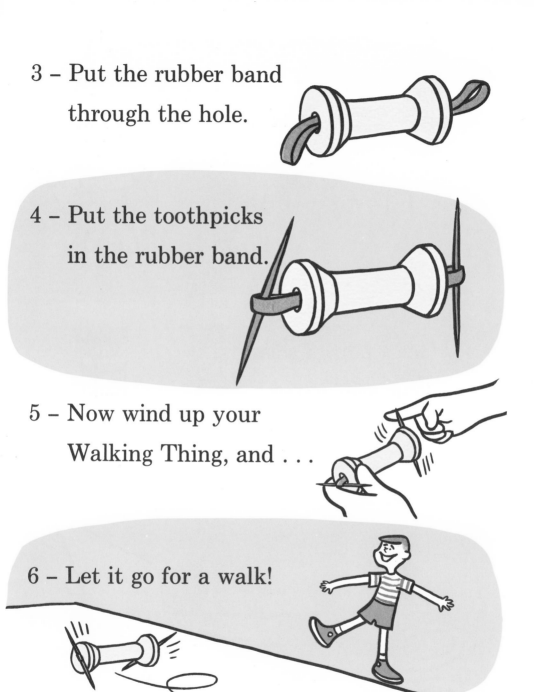

4 – Put the toothpicks
   in the rubber band.

5 – Now wind up your
   Walking Thing, and . . .

6 – Let it go for a walk!

How to Make

a

Clompy Clown

1 – Get a pair of scissors,

   some stiff paper,

   and some crayons.

2 – Draw a clown
   and cut him out.

3 – Now color him.

   Make him funny!

4 – Cut out two holes

   for his legs.

5 – He can run!

   He can dance!

Why not make two of them?

How to Make
Ding Dong Music

1 – Ask your mother for four old glasses and a wooden spoon.

2 – Put this much water in one glass.

3 – Put this much in another glass.

4 – Put this much
in the next glass.

5 – Put this much
in the last one.

6 – Stand the glasses
in front of you
like this.

7 – Tap them.
Don't hit them
too hard.

Play along with the music
from your radio or TV.

How to Make

a

Link Link Chain

1 – Get some paper,
   some scissors,
   and some glue.

2 – Cut the paper
   in strips like this.

3 – Stick one piece
   in a ring like this.

4 – Put another piece
   in the ring like this.

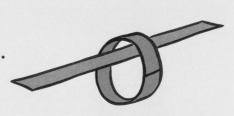

5 – Then stick that
   one together.

6 – Stick another and another
   and another and another.

Maybe you can make
a chain half a mile long!

How to Make
a
Spud Bunny

1 – You need a potato.
Toothpicks. Glue. Paper.
Scissors. Paper cup.
Three thumbtacks.

2 – Cut two big feet.
Cut two big ears.
Glue a toothpick
onto each ear.

3 – Stick a toothpick
into the potato.

4 – Push this toothpick
into the cup.
Glue the feet
on the cup.

5 – Push toothpicks
in for whiskers.

6 – Push the tacks in
for eyes and nose.
Push in the ears.

Now make the Spud Bunny's sister.

How to Grow

a

Goofy Garden

1 – Get a deep dish

and some

pretty little stones.

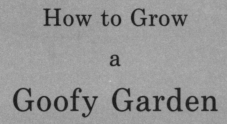

2 – Now get two carrots.

Eat them.

But save the tops.

3 – Put the stones
in the dish.
Pour some water
on the stones.

4 – Cut the carrot
tops like this.
Then put them
on the stones.

5 – Keep those stones wet.

Watch your
Goofy Garden grow.

How to Make

a

Tippy Top

1 – Get a piece of paper,
a glass and a pencil.
Scissors. Crayon.
Also a toothpick.

2 – Put the glass
on the paper.
Draw around it
with the pencil.

3 – Now cut out the
circle you made.
Draw this on it.

4 – Push the toothpick
through the center
of the paper.

5 – Give it a spin!
Spin it on a table.

How to Make
a
Parachute

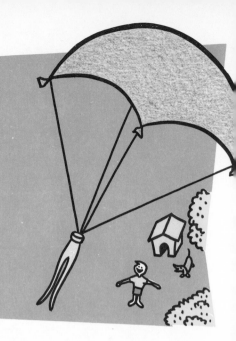

1 – Ask your mother
   for a paper napkin,
   some thread, and
   a clothespin.

2 – Cut four pieces
   of thread,
   all two feet long.

3 – Tie the thread
   to the corners
   of the napkin.

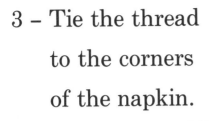
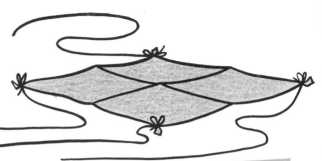

4 – Tie the ends
   of the threads together.
   Then tie them
   to the clothespin.

5 – Lay it all out
   very straight
   and roll it up.

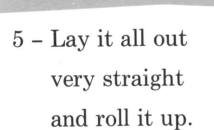

Throw it as high
as you can.
But not in the house!

How to Make

a

Two-horned Noser

1 – Get a small paper bag,

crayons and scissors.

2 – Draw a face on the bag.

Make it a funny face.

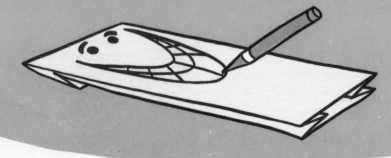

3 – Cut two holes in
the top of the bag,
and one where the
nose goes.

4 – Put your hand
in the bag.
Put one finger
in each hole.

5 – Now wiggle your horns
and waggle your nose.

How to Make
a
Wind Thing

1 – Get four paper cups,
   a piece of cardboard,
   some stickum, a bead,
   a pin, and a stick.

2 – Draw two lines
   on the cardboard
   like this.

3 – Now stick a cup
   on each corner
   with stickum.

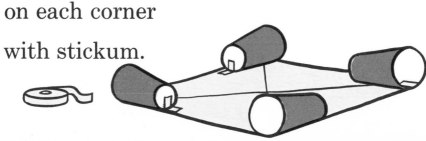

4 – Put the pin in
   the cardboard
   where the two
   lines cross.

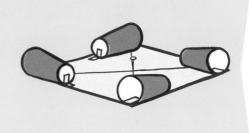

5 – Put the pin
   through the bead.
   Tap the pin
   into the stick.

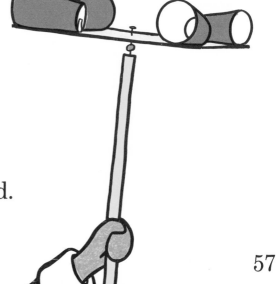

Now take it outside
and look for some wind.

How to Make
Birds Happy

1 – Get a milk box,
scissors and
some string.

2 – Ask your dad
to cut the box
like this.

3 – Have him make
   a hole here.

4 – Put the string
   through the hole.

5 – Put little pieces of bread
   in the bottom of the box.

6 – Hang it up
   in a tree.

Now your birds
will have a lunchroom!

How to Make

a

Moogle Mask

1 – You need a paper bag.

The biggest bag you can get.

2 – Draw a funny face

on the bag.

Cut two holes

for the eyes.

3 – Stick a paper cup

on for a nose.

4 – Cut out some hair.
Stick it on.

5 – Cut out some glasses.
Stick them on.

6 – Now put on your mask.

None of your friends
will know who you are!